Papa

I love you
because

I Love You Because Books
www.riverbreezepress.com

To Papa

Love, _____

Date: _____

The best thing about you is your

_____

Thank you for being patient with me when

_____

You are better than a

_____

You should win the grand prize for

_____

You make me feel special when

_____

Papa, I love you more than

I love when you tell me about

_____

I love when we

_____

together

You taught me how to

_____

I know you love me because

_____

I wish I could

---

as well as
you do

Papa, I love that we have the same

You should be the king of

_____

You have an amazing talent for

_____

Papa, you make me laugh when you

_____

I wish I had more time to

_____

with you

You make the best

_____

You have
inspired me to

_____

If I could give
you anything it
would be

_____

I would love to go

_____

with you

You are
there for me when

_____

Papa, I love you because you are

_____

Made in the USA
Monee, IL
07 May 2022

96062665R00031